FOOD and FARMING

FEEDING
the WORLD

Richard and Louise Spilsbury

PowerKiDS
press™
New York

Published in 2011 by The Rosen Publishing Group Inc.
29 East 21st Street, New York, NY 10010

First Edition

Editor: Julia Adams
Managing Editor, Discovery Books: Rachel Tisdale
Editor, Discovery Books: Jenny Vaughan
Designer and illustrator: Graham Rich
Picture researcher: Bobby Humphrey
Consultant: Nicholas Rowles

Library of Congress Cataloging-in-Publication Data

Spilsbury, Richard, 1963-
    Feeding the world / by Richard and Louise Spilsbury. — 1st ed.
        p. cm. — (Food and farming)
    Includes index.
    ISBN 978-1-61532-579-5 (library binding)
    ISBN 978-1-61532-587-0 (paperback)
    ISBN 978-1-61532-588-7 (6-pack)
    1. Agriculture—Juvenile literature. 2. Agricultural productivity—Juvenile literature.
    3. Food supply—Juvenile literature. I. Spilsbury, Louise. II. Title. III. Series: Food and farming.
    S519.S72 2010
    630—dc22
                                                    2009045754

Photographs:
CFW Images: pp. 13 (Edward Parker/EASI Images), 28 (John Birdsall); Istockphoto.com:
pp. 11 top right, 11 top (Bill Grove); Getty Images: pp. 5 (Peter Busomoke), 10 (Stuart Fox),
14 (Harald Sund), 17 (Chris Whitehead), 22 (Liu Yonghao/China Photos), 23 (Jerry Kobalenko),
25 & title page (Michael Spencer), 27 (STR/AFP); Make Poverty History: p. 29; Shutterstock:
pp. 6 (Losevsky Pavel), 9 (Hannu Liivaar), 16 (Keith Naylor), 18 & front cover top (ene),
21 (Lee Torrens)

Manufactured in China
CPSIA Compliance Information: Batch #WAS0102PK: For Further Information
contact Rosen Publishing, New York, New York at 1-800-237-9932

CONTENTS

FOOD CRISIS

Today, there is a crisis in world food and the poorest people on Earth are struggling to get enough to eat. One of the main reasons for this is that the cost of food rises if farmers have to pay more for the resources they need to grow it.

Oil

One of the most important resources that farmers use is, as in many other industries, oil. When the price of oil is high, this raises the price of food. This is because oil is needed to run machines, and many chemicals used in farming are made from oil. The cost of fuel used by vehicles delivering food also gets higher, making food in stores more expensive. Since oil costs so much, many farmers are growing grain crops such as corn to make into fuel, which we call "biofuel." If they do this instead of growing food, food becomes more expensive.

Unfair Trade

Governments of rich countries sometimes pay their farmers to produce cheap food, to keep them in business. Payments from governments

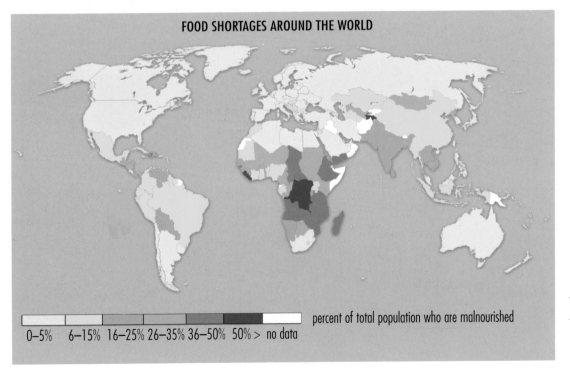

FOOD SHORTAGES AROUND THE WORLD

percent of total population who are malnourished

0–5% 6–15% 16–25% 26–35% 36–50% 50% > no data

◄ *This map shows where there are high percentages of people who do not have enough to eat.*

▲ *Kenyans displaced by conflict—the result of competition for fertile land—line up for food. Food shortages are frequently the result of political upheaval that can often be traced to poverty.*

to farmers in rich countries add up to over $1 billion every day! They may insist the poor countries open their markets to this cheap food. Selling all over the world in this way is called "globalization." Local farmers cannot compete with the cheap food and may not be able to continue farming. As a result, less food is grown. Unfair trade agreements make things worse. Poor countries may agree to buy materials they need to grow food from rich countries. In return, they agree to sell the rich countries the food they grow, at whatever price the rich countries will pay. This interdependence can mean that farmers may find they can only afford to go on growing food if they get aid from rich countries. The aid takes the form of fertilizers, machinery, and even food.

DEBATE

Should We Eat Less Meat?

As people in some parts of the world become wealthier, they eat more meat. For example, meat consumption in China doubled between 1990 and 2005. Scientists estimate that 600 million tons of grain is fed to livestock each year—enough to feed a billion people. Argentinian farmers export millions of tons of soybeans each year for cattle feed. But half the country's population cannot afford enough food.

FARMING FOOD

In rich countries, many farms are big businesses. They grow vast amounts of crops—often of just a few types. The farmers make their money by selling their crops and use this to buy everything they need to keep their farms going, and to feed themselves and their families.

In and Out

Large-scale farms can often produce very cheap food—especially if they get government help to keep them in business. Farmers grow a wide range of foods using different farming methods. These include, for example, intensive farming, where a large amount of food is produced in a small space, extensive, where much more space is used, and other kinds of small- and large-scale farming. All methods of farming are done using the same basic system. All farms need inputs. Farming inputs include labor, as well as money to buy farm machines,

◄ *Supermarkets buy large quantities of food from large-scale food producers, all over the world. Often, they pay the lowest price possible. This is popular with customers, but may cause hardship for farmers.*

seeds, and animals. They also depend on processes. These include the different jobs farmers must do, such as plowing, sowing, adding fertilizer to the soil, milking cows, and harvesting crops. The processes lead to outputs, which are the food grown, and also any waste products.

starvation and others may suffer from malnutrition, which means not getting enough food to stay healthy. The major reason for world hunger is poverty. Poverty has a number of causes—and can include unfair trade agreements, and countries not being able to compete in a global market. Poor farmers may not have money for farm tools or fertilizer, or enough good land to grow food, and little money to buy food if their crops fail. As world food prices increase, world hunger is likely to get worse.

World Hunger

Modern farms can produce large quantities of food, but over 850 million people worldwide do not have enough to eat. Some face

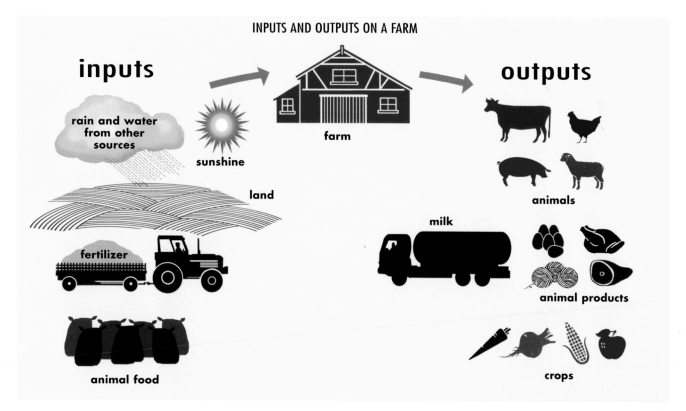

INPUTS AND OUTPUTS ON A FARM

inputs

rain and water from other sources

sunshine

land

farm

fertilizer

animal food

outputs

animals

milk

animal products

crops

▲ *Farming depends on inputs to get outputs. Inputs are everything farmers need to grow crops and rear animals. Outputs are the crops, the animals, and the products made using these, such as milk and meat from the animals.*

WHERE FOOD GROWS

Different places have different growing conditions. These include the amount of rainfall or sunlight, the type of soil, and the slope of the land.

Growing Conditions

Crops produce the best output (they grow better) in regions where the growing conditions suit their needs best. For instance, banana trees grow well in tropical places, where the weather is warm and wet. Wheat grows best on flat land in climates that are warm (but not too hot) and dry in summer. Countries depend on being able to buy food they cannot grow from countries where it can be produced. This is global trade.

Controlling Conditions

Many farmers change the natural growing conditions on their farms to maximize (get the best of) their output, and to produce a large amount of food at low prices. This means getting the largest amount of crops, and the best quality. For example, they irrigate or add water artificially to soil that does not receive enough rainfall for crops to grow. Farmers dig ditches, ponds, or even cut ledges into hillsides to hold onto any rainwater that falls. They may add fertilizer to soil that does not have enough nutrients (useful chemicals that help plants grow) to produce healthy crops. Farmers often grow crops in greenhouses. These structures trap the sun's heat to make growing conditions inside warmer than outside.

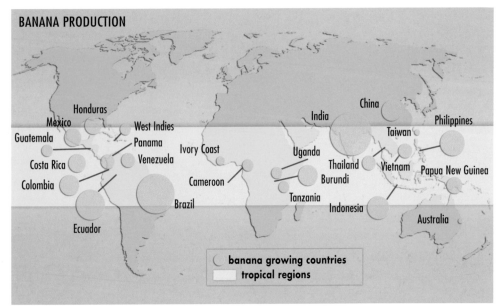

BANANA PRODUCTION

Honduras
Mexico
Guatemala
West Indies
Costa Rica
Panama
Colombia
Venezuela
Ivory Coast
Cameroon
Brazil
Ecuador
China
India
Uganda
Thailand
Burundi
Tanzania
Indonesia
Philippines
Taiwan
Vietnam
Papua New Guinea
Australia

◐ banana growing countries
▢ tropical regions

◀ *This world map shows a light-colored band, which covers the tropics—the part of the world where the climate is mostly warm all year. Where it is wet as well as warm, bananas grow well, and the map also shows the countries where large quantities of bananas grow. Farmers in these places depend on being able to sell their bananas for a good price, in order to buy foods they cannot grow, as well as other things they need.*

The Rain in Spain

In southern Spain, there are huge areas of greenhouses. Here, farmers grow salad crops, such as tomatoes and lettuces. They sell these throughout the rest of Europe. Farming in the greenhouses provides work for many people. However, southern Spain has a naturally very dry climate, and salad crops need lots of water to grow. The Spanish government supplies water cheaply to farmers for irrigation, so their input costs are not too high. But using up local water for irrigation has created water shortages for some communities in the region.

▼ These greenhouses in Spain grow large quantities of salad crops.
The winter climate in Spain is not warm enough to grow them outdoors,
but the greenhouses make it possible to grow the crops all year.

FARMING FOR THE FAMILY

About half of all the people in the world eat only, or almost only, the food they can grow for themselves and their families. This is called subsistence farming. This is the most common type of farming in parts of Africa and Asia.

Struggle for Survival

In subsistence farming, the input of labor is high. People work hard, using only simple tools to dig, plant crops, and clear land of weeds. The input of money and equipment (tools) is very low. The output on a subsistence farm depends almost entirely on the climate. In good years, when there is enough rainfall, there may be more food than the family needs. We say this is a surplus. Farmers can sell some of the surplus to pay for new seeds or livestock and other things they need. They may also be able to store food for the future. In bad years, families may struggle to survive. Crops may fail if there is not enough rain, leaving people with little food and no money to buy any from stores.

◀ Many Africans grow food largely for their own use—as in this vegetable plot in South Africa. Sometimes, a little is left over to sell in local markets.

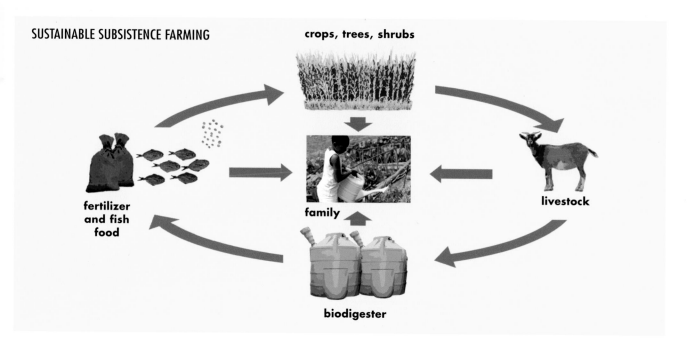

SUSTAINABLE SUBSISTENCE FARMING

crops, trees, shrubs

fertilizer and fish food

family

livestock

biodigester

▲ *Families living on subsistence farms eat the food from their crops and animals, and make use of waste products to produce gas for cooking, fish food, and fertilizer. All this helps them produce more food at low cost, with little waste. This is sustainable farming.*

If their animals get sick, subsistence farmers may not be able to afford animal medicines or vet's fees, so there is always the danger that their livestock may die from sickness or injury.

> ❝ *God determines how much food I have to eat. I can only pray for good rains.* ❞
>
> Mary Sampuo, subsistence farmer, Zambia.

Zero Waste

On subsistence farms, farmers do not have money for expensive fertilizers to enrich (improve) the soil. Instead, they use farm waste to create more farm output. For example, they use some crop waste to feed livestock, and some livestock dung to help fertilize the soil, wasting almost nothing.

CASE STUDY

Biodigesters

In some parts of the world, such as China and Vietnam, farmers use biodigesters. These are special tanks where farmers put leftover farm waste. Tiny organisms called bacteria turn the waste into biogas, which people can burn as fuel to cook food and heat or light their homes. Sludge from the biodigester trickles into a pond where it feeds fish the people can eat, or it can be used as fertilizer. This helps the farm run sustainably, which means that there is little waste and the farmer does not have to buy any fertilizer.

HIGH-INPUT FARMING

In rich countries, many farmers use high inputs and resources to get a high output of food. This is called intensive farming. Intensive farms often grow large amounts of single crops, such as rice, tomatoes, grapes, or oranges.

Inputs on Intensive Farms

Intensive farms produce a lot of food, sometimes from small areas of land. The farmers often add fertilizers to soil to make plants grow better, and so that they can grow crops repeatedly on the same fields. They spray the crops with chemicals called insecticides that kill insects that might otherwise damage crops. Farmers may install large networks of pipes to bring water to the fields to irrigate the crops. Intensive farming also requires large amounts of energy resources, including fuel for tractors and electricity for irrigation pumps.

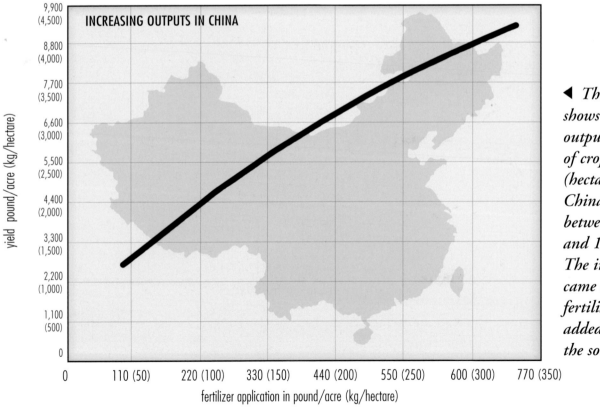

INCREASING OUTPUTS IN CHINA

yield pound/acre (kg/hectare)

9,900 (4,500)
8,800 (4,000)
7,700 (3,500)
6,600 (3,000)
5,500 (2,500)
4,400 (2,000)
3,300 (1,500)
2,200 (1,000)
1,100 (500)
0

fertilizer application in pound/acre (kg/hectare)

0 110 (50) 220 (100) 330 (150) 440 (200) 550 (250) 600 (300) 770 (350)

◀ *This graph shows how the output (yield) of crops per acre (hectare) in China increased between 1952 and 1993. The increase came as fertilizer was added to the soil.*

▲ *Vast fields of intensively grown crops, such as these soybeans in Brazil, need to be irrigated (watered) by machine, which is costly in terms of fuel and water.*

Intensive Problems

Intensive farming can increase the productivity of the land, but it can cause problems. Irrigation may use up water resources, leaving less for the people in the area. Farm workers can get sick from touching or breathing in farm chemicals, and this damage to their health can be permanent. The soil becomes impoverished after crops are grown on it year in and year out. More and more artificial fertilizer may be needed, adding to the farmers' costs. Rain washes fertilizers from the soil into rivers, causing pollution that harms wildlife, and may even affect the water supplies to people's homes.

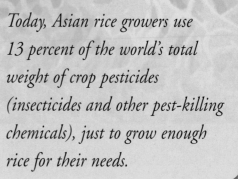

PESTICIDES

Today, Asian rice growers use 13 percent of the world's total weight of crop pesticides (insecticides and other pest-killing chemicals), just to grow enough rice for their needs.

GROWING STAPLE FOODS

Staple foods are the main foods that people in a particular part of the world eat. Staple foods are rich in carbohydrates, which our bodies use to give us energy.

Wheat Fields

The most common global staples are cereal crops, such as wheat, corn, and rice. They became common since they were not expensive to buy and were filling to eat. Farmers in rich countries often grow wheat in enormous fields. Wheat grows best in areas with fertile soil and temperate climates where there is not too much rainfall. Major wheat-growing areas include central North America and northern China. With the right growing conditions, the crops do not need much input of fertilizer, irrigation, and labor. The output of grain from the tens of thousands of plants in the large fields is high. This is extensive farming. Wheat farmers in rich countries use machines to cut down on labor. For example, they may spray insecticides onto crops from aircraft.

Different Staples

People in different parts of the world eat different staple foods. In much of Asia, it is rice. In most of Africa, corn is a staple although, in some areas, the major staples are not grains, but roots such as yams and cassava. They may even be plantains (a kind of banana). A favorite staple in Ethiopia is the grain teff, which is used to make a kind of pancake. Teff produces tiny, highly nutritious grains. Unfortunately, teff is expensive to produce and Ethiopians often have to make do with cheaper grains.

◀ *The huge farms of North America provide much of the world's wheat. The farm machinery needed to harvest such vast areas has to be large. Very often, several combine harvesters are used at once in order to gather in as much of the crop as possible in the short time that it is at its best.*

▼ These Thai farmers are tending a rice field. More than 90 percent of the world's rice is grown and consumed in Asia, where it is the most important staple food. Poor people in the region may spend as much as three-quarters of their income on rice. If the harvest is poor, or prices rise for some other reason, millions of people can suffer.

Many farmers throughout the world grow food for sale without using artificial chemicals such as fertilizers. This is called organic farming.

Natural Fertility

Many people buy organic food because they believe that chemicals make the food less healthy. Another reason they prefer these foods is that they worry about the damage that chemicals can do to natural environments. Organic farmers use natural ways to increase soil fertility, such as adding manure or compost. Compost is rotted down plant waste. They also grow quick-growing plants such as clover, alfalfa, and mustard on their fields. These plants are sometimes called green manure, because the farmers plow them into the soil to add nutrients to it.

▲ *Organic farmers often grow plants that encourage insect-eating pests. For example, nettles attract ladybugs. These feed on aphids, which are crop pests.*

▲ *Compost, made from rotted plant waste, and manure are both natural fertilizers that can improve the soil and make crops grow better.*

Taking Turns

Organic farmers often use crop rotation to keep their soil healthy. This means varying which plants they grow on each section of their land. This helps to keep the soil fertile, as some crops, such as beans, help add nutrients to the soil. It also makes sure insects and other pests attracted to the crop do not build up in the fields. For example, they grow potatoes on a field one year, onions and carrots the next, then beans and peas, and finally, cabbages.

WEEDS & PESTS

Like all farmers, organic farmers need to control weeds and pests, which can reduce output. They sometimes get rid of crop pests using safer sprays such as derris, which is made from plant roots.

ANIMAL FARMING

Livestock are animals that farmers rear and sell for their meat and eggs. Cattle, sheep, goats, pigs, and buffalo are all livestock. So are hens, ducks, turkeys, and even, sometimes, ostriches.

Rich and Poor

Livestock farming is practiced in much of the world, but the kinds of animals farmed and the conditions they are kept in differ according to local customs and the kind of meat people prefer to eat. The way the animals are reared also differs. In poor countries, there may be just a few animals, in rich countries, many more. Livestock provide us with meat, which is an important source of protein. Protein is a

▲ *Keeping large numbers of poultry, such as these turkeys, in very crowded conditions means that huge amounts of meat can be produced very cheaply.*

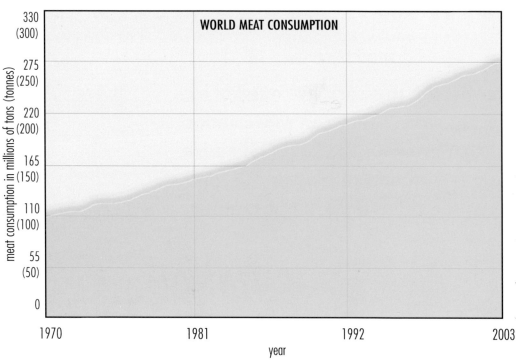

WORLD MEAT CONSUMPTION

meat consumption in millions of tons (tonnes)

330 (300)
275 (250)
220 (200)
165 (150)
110 (100)
55 (50)
0

1970 1981 1992 2003

year

◀ *This graph shows how world meat consumption rose between 1970 and 2003. The greatest increase has been in countries that were poor in the past and are becoming wealthier, and where their populations have risen, making the demand for meat greater.*

substance in food that our bodies need to grow and remain strong. But livestock needs a lot of animal feed to grow, which makes it expensive. It takes at least seven pounds of grain to produce one pound of beef. There are other, cheaper sources of protein, such as beans. In rich countries, animal products such as meat make up around one-third of people's diets. In Sierra Leone, in Africa, it is seven percent.

Animal Factories

On intensive livestock farms, large numbers of animals are kept together, often inside buildings. Here, they are fed on grain and protein-rich feed so they grow meat or lay eggs fast. Farmers give the animals medicines to keep them healthy but also to make them grow as big as possible. This is sometimes called "factory farming." It is a way of supplying large quantities of cheap meat, using high-input methods. Factory farms can meet the growing demand for meat.

CASE STUDY

Pig Farms–U.S.-Style

The biggest pig factory farms in the United States are home to hundreds of thousands of pigs. Pigs live their whole lives in barns with 25 pens, each with 20 pigs inside. Machines supply water and food automatically and also control the temperature in the barns. The pigs are ready to be killed for meat after six months. Some farms may produce a million pigs every two weeks.

FREEDOM OR FACTORY?

On free-range farms, the livestock live outside in fields and ranches, where they can move about and feed on plants that grow on the land. This type of extensive farming is common in places with lots of grassland not used for any other kind of farming.

Free-range

Free-range animals take up more space than those in factory farms, so there is lower output of meat from each field. However, farmers spend less on inputs such as feed and chemicals. Free-range farming can mean animals are healthier. In factory farms, if one animal catches a disease, others will probably get it, too. For instance, some scientists believe that the disease bird flu (which can spread to people) may have been made worse by giving chemicals to factory-farmed poultry, and so reducing their resistance to disease, which spreads easily in crowded conditions. In some countries, many people prefer to eat meat from free-range farms because they believe it is less cruel than intensive farming.

Environmental Issues

However, extensive farming causes problems of its own. In some parts of the world, farmers have destroyed large areas of tropical forest to create space for ranches. Also, free-ranging livestock, such as goats, can trample soil and eat up so many plants that the land in dry areas may turn to desert where almost no crops can grow.

CASE STUDY

Rain Forest Beef

Since 1960, over one third of the Brazilian rain forest has been destroyed, often to make way for cattle ranches. Grasses growing on cleared tropical soil take up the nutrients. Once cattle have eaten the grass, the soil has few nutrients left, and land that was once forest becomes almost useless.

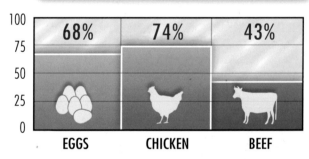

▲ *This chart shows the percentages of eggs, chicken, and beef that are produced throughout the world using intensive farming.*

▼ Extensive livestock farming, such as on this sheep farm in New Zealand, needs space and plenty of grass and wild plants for animals to graze on. New Zealand has a small human population and plenty of space to rear sheep under these conditions.

DAIRY FARMING

Many people worldwide collect milk from their livestock, to drink or to make into dairy products, such as cheese and yogurt. The most commonly produced milk is from cows, but people also use goat, sheep, yak, buffalo, and camel milk.

World Milk

There are over 225 million dairy cows in the world, producing over 500 million tons of milk each year. Most milk is produced in India, the U.S.A., Western Europe, and New Zealand. In some parts of South America, Africa, and Asia, people traditionally do not drink much milk or eat milk products.

▼ *In a modern milking parlor, large numbers of cows can be milked automatically by machine, all at the same time. This is both quick and hygienic, but machinery is only available in wealthy countries.*

Fields and Sheds

In poor parts of the world, farmers may keep only a few cows, and usually milk them by hand. However, dairy farming in richer places is often an intensive farming system. Dairy farmers may have herds of several hundreds of cows in their fields. They use milking machines set up in milking parlors to get the milk from the cows, and refrigerated tanks to keep it fresh. In some places, cows graze in open fields for much of the year, and come to the farm for milking twice a day. Elsewhere, cows remain in or near sheds with concrete floors for most of their lives. Farmers feed the cows on high-protein feed, so they produce as much milk as possible.

▲ For many desert-dwelling people, camels provide for a variety of needs, most importantly transportation and, as shown here, in Turkmenistan, milk.

HOLSTEINS

The Holstein is the most common dairy cow breed in the U.S.A. and Europe. This is because it produces a large amount of milk. A single cow can produce up to 16 gallons (60 L) of milk a day, or 6,870 gallons (26,000 L) in a lifetime. This is ten times the amount a cow needs to feed her calves, so there is plenty for dairy farmers to sell.

FISH FARMING

The fastest growing type of farming worldwide is fish farming. Around 85 percent of fish farming takes place in poor countries, mostly in parts of Asia and South America.

Fish Inputs

Farmed fish include carp and salmon, kept in ponds or in cages in rivers or the sea. Farmers also produce shellfish, including shrimp, or prawns, in seawater ponds. Fish farming can produce a high output of fast-growing fish, a food type that is rich in protein. The inputs that fish farms need are space, water, and feed. In some places, farmers are destroying coastal forests to create fish farms. Some crop farmers also convert their fields into fish farms, because farmed fish can be sold for more money than crops. In some places, it is possible to practice more extensive kinds of fish farming. This means keeping fish in their natural habitat, sometimes providing them with a little extra food, but usually, doing little more than protecting them from predators. Extensive fish farms raise fewer fish in their space than intensive farms. However, raising fish in this

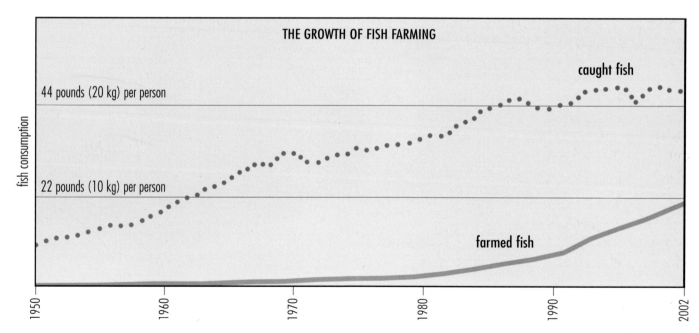

▲ *In the last 50 years, more of the fish eaten in the world has come from farms, though much is still caught in the wild.*

▲ *Shrimp farming (also called prawn farming) is a major source of income in many parts of the world. Here, farmers off the coast of Thailand raise shrimp for sale all over the world.*

way can be cheaper than intensive methods, because the farmers do not need to provide the fish with much food. This kind of fish farming has been practiced for centuries in northern Italy.

Fish Food

Feed for farmed fish is often made from small, wild ocean fish such as anchovies and sand eels. So many of these fish are caught for use in fish farming that there is less food for other marine animals to eat, leading to a drop in the numbers of wild fish.

CASE STUDY

Asian Shrimp Farms

In Asian countries such as Thailand, shrimp farming is common. The farmers often create shallow ponds for shrimp larvae to grow in. These feed on plants and animals in the water, or on the feed farmers buy. It takes three to six months for the larvae to grow into adult shrimp.

CASH CROPS

A cash crop is grown for sale, often to other countries. The term is often applied to crops grown on plantations (very large farms) or small farms in poor countries mainly to sell to rich countries. Typical cash crops include coffee, tea, cocoa, bananas, and soybeans.

A Single Crop

In some parts of the world, cash cropping is the major type of farming. For example, there are many coffee plantations in Brazil, because the conditions there suit coffee plants well. One of the dangers for a farmer growing cash crops is that his or her livelihood is linked too closely to what happens to a single crop. Bad weather may destroy it, or businesses in foreign countries may decide to pay less for coffee beans or buy from a completely different cash cropping area. If this happens, many farmers in a coffee-growing region may be ruined.

Fair Trade

The Fair Trade movement began because many people in rich countries wanted to make sure poor farmers got a fair price for their produce. Fair Trade means farmers growing cash crops get a fair price for their output, regardless of changes in world prices. People pay a little extra for Fair Trade food than normally produced cash crops. In exchange, they know that the farmers have safe and good working conditions. Farming communities also get paid extra money to improve social and environmental conditions.

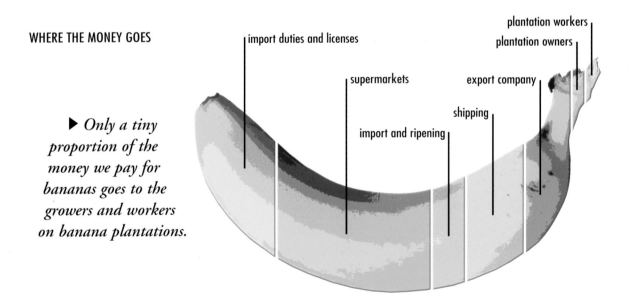

WHERE THE MONEY GOES

import duties and licenses

supermarkets

import and ripening

shipping

export company

plantation owners

plantation workers

▶ *Only a tiny proportion of the money we pay for bananas goes to the growers and workers on banana plantations.*

CASE STUDY

Windward Islands Bananas

More than 90 percent of all bananas grown in the Windward Isles, West Indies, are Fair Trade. The extra money from Fair Trade has paid for hospital equipment, a computer laboratory for local people, school facilities, and new roads. Banana farmers are also supplied with trees to grow on sloping land to stop soil washing away. The bananas can be grown on this soil in the future.

◀ *Soybeans are an important source of protein for cattle and people. They are grown in large quantities in South America, but often, the people actually working on the land get very little money for their work.*

HOW TO FEED THE WORLD

Farmers are growing enough food to feed the world. But it is not reaching the poorest people. Political changes between countries and within countries can help solve this. So can changes in the way farmers grow food.

▲ *This woman is watering plants in a kitchen garden in Cuba. Small-scale farms like this can provide valuable sources of food for people who otherwise might be unable to afford enough good food.*

Trade Not Aid

Governments of rich countries make agreements with poor countries to help their farmers trade food globally. This globalization of trade can help poorer countries get richer—but only if the trade agreements involved are fair. Fair Trade production can also help. It means that poorer countries need less aid to make sure their populations develop better living standards.

Making the Best of the Land

Farmers need to avoid harming the environment. This will ensure good food supply into the future. Sustainable farming is a way farmers can do this. For instance, farmers in dry climates can use sustainable methods to grow more crops per drop of water by irrigating carefully, and by choosing drought-resistant varieties. A good way to encourage sustainable farming is for poor people to own or have access to good farmland, which they will want to care for. Land not used for farming in the past could also be brought into production. For example, in Cuba's capital city, Havana, farmers grow vegetables intensively and organically on small city farms.

▲ On July 2, 2005, around 225,000 people demonstrated on the streets of Edinburgh, in Scotland, calling on the leaders of the world's richest countries, who were meeting in Scotland, to end world poverty. Their slogan was "Make Poverty History." Sadly, many people throughout the world remain in poverty, despite such campaigns.

DEBATE

Can Growing GM Crops Help End World Hunger?

GM stands for Genetically Modified. It refers to crops that have been altered by scientists to produce higher yields, contain extra nutrients, or be better able to withstand pest attacks. Some people believe that these could combat world hunger. Others fear that they could harm the environment. For example, some GM crops are designed to withstand large doses of herbicides, so weeds in fields can be destroyed, but the chemicals may harm other organisms. Another problem is that the companies producing these seeds often try to prevent farmers from saving some of their crop to re-plant the next year. Poor farmers have always done this to save money, but some companies want to make it illegal. This is so that the companies can sell more seeds and become richer.

GLOSSARY

carbohydrate a major nutrient (useful substance in food). It is found in foods containing sugar or starch, such as grains and potatoes, and gives us energy.

cash crop a crop grown chiefly for sale, not for the farmer's own use, and often not for the use of the community around the farm, either. Cash crops are often grown on a large scale in many poor countries and are sold abroad. They include tea, coffee, and sugar.

climate the average pattern of weather in a place over several years. For example, somewhere with a warm climate has warm weather much of the time, but not necessarily always.

dairy product milk, and foods made from milk, including yogurt, cheese, and butter. Most of the world's dairy products are made from cows' milk.

deprivation a lack of food and other necessities of life.

extensive farming producing single crops such as wheat, or certain kinds of livestock, over large areas of land.

Fair Trade a movement supported by campaigners against poverty, which tries to make sure that farmers in poor countries get a fair deal when they sell their produce.

fertilizer man-made chemical or natural substance such as animal dung used to improve the quality and quantity of plant growth.

free-range animals that are allowed to roam outdoors in large fields.

fuel anything that can be burned to make energy to heat homes, run machinery, and so on. Fuels used throughout the world include oil, gas, and wood.

input anything that is put into producing on a farm or in a factory. On a farm, inputs will include the labor (work) needed to grow crops, fertilizer to improve the soil, seeds, and so on.

insecticides chemicals used to kill insects that attack crops. Many can harm other animals if they are eaten in large quantities.

intensive in farming, this means putting in a lot of labor and inputs such as fertilizer to get a large output—more than the land would produce naturally. Intensively farmed foods include greenhouse-grown salads and battery-farm eggs.

interdependence depending on each other—when two sets of people or things depend on each other to work properly.

irrigate supply dry farmland with water, using pipes, pumps, and sprayers. It often means drawing water from rivers or from wells that reach deep under the ground.

livestock animals that farmers keep to supply meat, wool, or other outputs. The word is usually applied to cattle, sheep, and goats.

malnutrition not getting enough of the right kinds of food the body needs to stay healthy. Even people who get plenty to eat may be malnourished if their food does not contain all the nutrients they need.

nutrients substances that help living things to grow healthily. Good soil contains nutrients to help plants grow, and fertilizers add more nutrients. People and animals get nutrients from food.

organic farming farming without using man-made chemicals, such as fertilizers or insecticides, or GM crops. It requires more labor than farming that uses modern techniques, but many people believe the food produced is tastier and healthier.

output products of a farm or a factory—in the case of a farm, it is the food produced.

plantation a large farm where cash crops, such as sugar, cotton, and tea, are grown.

process the activities done to produce an output. In farming, these include plowing, planting seeds, and adding fertilizer and water to the land.

protein type of nutrient found in foods such as meat and milk. Proteins are important for building strong, healthy bodies.

shellfish animals with shells that live in water, for example, crabs, shrimp, mussels, and oysters. They are not really fish.

staple food main food that people eat in order to provide them with energy. In much of the world, rice is the main staple.

subsistence farming using simple technology and few resources to produce enough food for the farmer's family, with little spare to trade.

surplus anything that is left over. In subsistence farming, surplus crops are those the farmer and his or her family do not need, which they can sell.

sustainable, sustainably using as few resources as possible and producing as little waste as possible, using natural pest control and fertilizer, by recycling and re-using waste.

system the way that any industry, including farming, works, with inputs and processes that lead to outputs.

TOPIC WEB, FIND OUT MORE, AND WEB SITES

FEEDING THE WORLD

Science and Environment

• Research the way plants, including crops, make their own food by photosynthesis. Draw a diagram to show the different steps in the process.
• Many farmers irrigate fields by raising water from rivers or lakes. Today, they use pumps but in the past some used the shadouf and Archimedes Screw. Find out how these machines work.
• Find out more about making a compost heap, and what happens in a compost heap to turn food and plant waste into fertilizer.

English and Literacy

• Write a letter to a local paper as though you are someone who objects to battery-produced eggs and chickens. Then write a farmer's reply, defending their choice to farm battery hens.
• Use history books, historical novels, and local resources to find out how people's diets have changed over the past 100 years. Create menus for different times in history to show how globalization has expanded our choice of food.

Geography

• Farming is not the only threat to tropical forests globally. Find out about the ways people are damaging forests and where the problems of deforestation are greatest. Draw a map to show the worst areas of deforestation.
• Research into the lives of the Maasai people of East Africa, who traditionally live by herding cattle. Look into the ways that modern science and technology is helping to improve their lives and that of their cattle.

History and Economics

• Research why and when Portuguese settlers first introduced oranges to South America.
• Find out about the slave trade between Europe, North America, and Africa that provided slave labor to farm cash crops including sugar, coffee, and cocoa.
• Investigate the workings of the Fair Trade movement. Create a poster showing the different ways in which Fair Trade has helped the economic development of farmers and their families.

Art and Culture

• Listen to traditional slavery songs from the U.S.A. and the Caribbean. What was life like for a slave on a plantation, and how do those working conditions compare to those on farms today?
• Artists who painted farming scenes include Jean-Francois Millet, Pieter Brueghel the Elder, and Pieter Brueghel the Younger. Search art books or art web sites to see their work and see what they tell you about farming methods in the past, and how they have changed.

FIND OUT MORE

Books

Deforestation Crisis
by Richard Spilsbury (Rosen Central, 2009)

Sustainable World: Food and Farming
by Rob Bowden (Kidshaven Press, 2003)

The Global Village: Food and Farming
by John Baines (Smart Apple Media, 2008)

Web Sites

Due to the changing nature of Internet links, PowerKids Press has developed an online list of Web sites related to the subject of this book. This site is updated regularly. Please use this link to access this list:
http://www.powerkidslinks.com/faf/world

INDEX